HAL LEONARD
GUITAR METHOD

SETUP & MAINTENANCE

Learn to Properly Adjust Your Guitar
for Peak Playability and Optimum Sound

BY CHAD JOHNSON

T0083885

ISBN 978-1-4584-1503-5

HAL•LEONARD®
CORPORATION
7777 W. BLUEMOUND RD. P.O. BOX 13819 MILWAUKEE, WI 53213

In Australia Contact:
Hal Leonard Australia Pty. Ltd.
4 Lentara Court
Cheltenham, Victoria, 3192 Australia
Email: ausadmin@halleonard.com.au

Visit Hal Leonard Online at
www.halleonard.com

DEDICATION

I'd like to dedicate this book to my late grandfathers, Ezra Grace Fowler and Edgar Hayes Johnson, my late uncle Charles Stafford Fowler, and to my father, Michael Wasmund Johnson, all of whom instilled in me the desire to build, repair, and tinker.

CONTENTS

INTRODUCTION

Welcome to the *Hal Leonard Guitar Setup and Maintenance Method*. This supplement to the *Hal Leonard Guitar Method* addresses a subject that's far-too-often neglected by guitarists of all levels: how to keep your guitars in top shape, inside and out. Many players, unduly afraid of making adjustments or repairs to their instruments, end up spending hard-earned money for someone else to do the job or, even worse, settling for a sub-par instrument. It may be hard to believe, but I've known players who've never even braved the pedestrian chore of changing their strings!

Of course, a healthy dose of caution is a good thing; there are certain instances where you can do real damage if you're not careful and well-informed. This book will make very clear which jobs should be handled by a qualified professional. However, *many* jobs, such as replacing a broken output jack, intonating, and adjusting the action, require little in the way of tools and only a modest skill set. With the information in this book, you'll be armed with the confidence and knowledge to tackle these chores and even more, if you're more of an adventurous type. Besides saving some green, you'll be rewarded with a great sense of accomplishment—not to mention a guitar that plays and sounds its best!

HOW TO USE THIS BOOK

While reading this book from cover to cover is certainly recommended, particularly for those new to the subject, this book is designed primarily as a reference. You may notice that certain bits of information are repeated in different chapters. This is done to avoid having to make awkward references to other chapters, in which the order of subjects may be different. Having self-contained chapters helps streamline the process and eliminates any source of possible confusion.

Having said that, feel free to read through the book in its entirety during your spare time, as it may spark some realizations and inspire some tinkering.

Note: This book is written according to a right-handed player's perspective. If you are left-handed, please reverse things with regards to right- and left-hand directions.

CHAPTER 1: GUITAR ANATOMY AND TOOLS

Before we start tweaking, let's make sure we're familiar with all the parts of a guitar. Many of you may know this already, but for those who don't, it's time to learn.

ACOUSTIC

Body: It's common for an acoustic guitar to use one wood for the top and another wood for the back and sides. The **soundhole** is found on the body.

Neck: The most common wood used on acoustics for the neck is rosewood.

Strings: Bronze strings are the most common for steel-string acoustics, whereas classical guitars use predominantly nylon strings.

Headstock: This is one of the ends where the strings are anchored.

Tuners: These are usually arranged three-to-a-side on an acoustic guitar.

Nut: Commonly made of bone, plastic, or a composite material, this little piece is a key factor in a well-playing guitar.

Fretboard: The thin strip of wood on the face of the neck is called the fretboard—most commonly rosewood or ebony on acoustics.

Frets: Frets come in different sizes, or gauges. The condition of the frets is important in a guitar's ability to both play in tune and produce a clear tone.

Inlays: These are commonly abalone or mother-of-pearl in both acoustic and electric guitars.

Bridge: The other ends of the strings are secured here, most commonly with bridge pins.

Saddle: Commonly made of bone, ivory, or plastic, this is the other point of contact (opposite the nut) for the string en route from the tuners to the bridge.

Pickguard: This protects the body of the guitar from pick scratches.

Strap buttons: If your acoustic has a pickup, the output jack is often combined with the strap button in the end block for a seamless appearance.

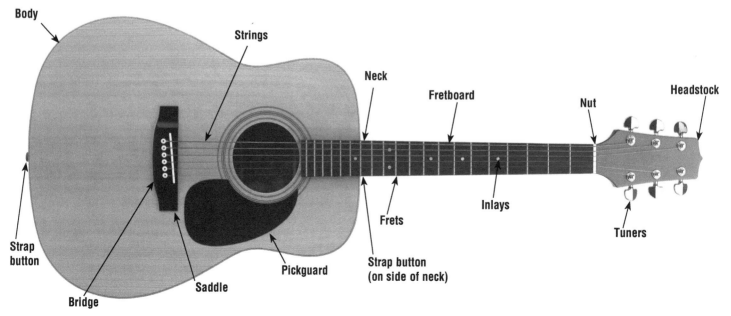

ELECTRIC

Body: Common woods for electrics include maple, alder, ash, and mahogany.

Neck: Maple and mahogany are most common on electric guitars.

Strings: Nickel and other alloys are commonly used for electric strings.

Headstock: This is one of the ends where the strings are anchored.

Tuners: These are found both in-line and three-to-a-side on electrics.

Nut: Commonly made of bone, plastic, or a composite material, this little piece is a key factor in a well-playing guitar.

Fretboard: This is most commonly rosewood, maple, or ebony on electrics.

Frets: Frets come in different sizes, or gauges. The condition of the frets is important in a guitar's ability to both play in tune and produce a clear tone.

Inlays: These are commonly abalone or mother-of-pearl in both acoustic and electric guitars.

Bridge: The other ends of the strings are secured here. There are various methods used for electric guitars, which we'll examine. If a guitar has a vibrato (whammy) bar, this is where it's mounted.

Pickguard: This protects the body of the guitar from pick scratches.

Pickups: The pickups sense the vibration of the strings and turn it into an electronic signal. There are two main types of electric pickups: single coils and humbuckers.

Tone and Volume Controls: These controls come in various configurations.

Pickup Selector: The most common selectors are 5-way or 3-way.

Output Jack: Commonly misnamed the *input jack*, this is where the electronic signal leaves your guitar, so it's important to keep it working properly.

Strap buttons: This is where you secure your strap.

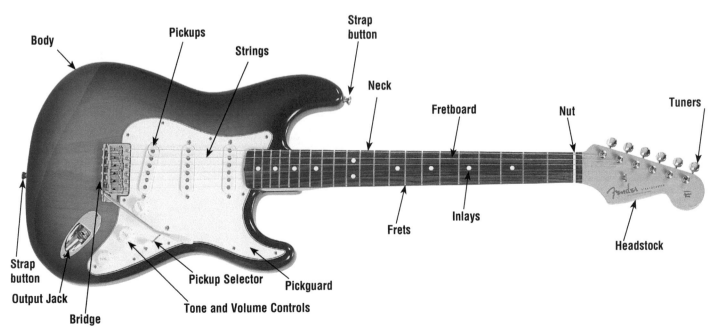

TOOLS OF THE TRADE

The following list of tools will handle over 95 percent of your typical setup and maintenance jobs. Most of these tools can serve several purposes, which saves not only money but also space in the workshop. If a more specific tool is required for a certain job, it will be indicated at the appropriate time.

Tuner: A strobe tuner is preferable, but a normal electric tuner will work.

Small Flashlight: This can help you see inside acoustics for various repairs.

Neck Rest: This "third hand" is invaluable for many jobs.

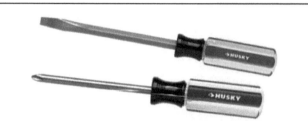

Screwdrivers (flathead and Phillips): These come in handy for all sorts of jobs.

Allen Wrenches: These are used mainly for adjusting truss rods and string saddles.

String Cutter: Wire cutters will work as well.

Nut Driver: Some truss rods require this tool, but it's also handy for other purposes as well, such as tightening an output jack.

String Winder (with bridge pin puller): When you're tuning up for the umpteenth time during a setup, you'll appreciate one of these.

Cleaner and Polisher: You'd be amazed the difference a good polish can make.

Capo: These come in handy when checking the neck.

6" Ruler: You'll use this for setting string height, among other things.

Precision Straightedge: This is necessary for checking the bow of the neck.

Feeler Gauges: For setting action and adjusting the neck, a set of feeler gauges is very handy. You'll probably have to order these online. They're not too expensive and they're very helpful in obtaining a quality setup.

Needle Nose Pliers: This is another handy tool with many uses.

Soldering Iron: You'll need one of these (and some solder) for electronic repairs or adjustments.

Solder Sucker or Desoldering Bulb: These come in handy for cleaning up solder blobs, which results in a neat appearance and usually a better connection.

Wire Strippers: If you're diving into the electronics, these are necessary.

WD-40 and/or DeOxit: These lubricants will help clean up rusted and dirty connections.

Nut Files: If you need to work on the nut, these are a must.

Sandpaper: You may need several different grades, depending on the job.

Tape Measure: This is another all-around good one to have around.

Hammer: This is useful when you get really frustrated. Instead of punching a hole through the wall, just take the hammer to it. (Just kidding.) These are useful for various jobs; you never know when a good tap is needed.

Keep in mind that you can purchase many of these tools as the need for them arises, and remember that you probably have several of these (such as a hammer, needle-nose pliers, etc.) lying around already.

Now that we know the difference between a saddle and a bridge, and a feeler gauge and a straightedge, it's time to start tweaking. Let's get to it!

CHAPTER 2: BASIC OPERATIONS

CHANGING STRINGS

It's truly unsettling to think that some players will take their guitars to a music store and pay up to $20 or more (including the price of strings) to have them restring it, but I have known several over the years. And I'm not talking about total beginners either; I'm talking about people who have been playing for years! Not only is restringing a guitar nothing to be afraid of—at all—it can actually be kind of fun and satisfying.

When changing strings, it makes things much easier if you have a place where you can lay the guitar down, such as a table or a workbench. Place a towel underneath the body, support the neck with a neck rest, and you're good to go. Though many a guitar has been restrung on a lap, bed, floor, or other surface, the job will be much more enjoyable if you're comfortable with adequate room to work.

ELECTRIC GUITARS

The first step is to remove the old strings. A quick way to do this is to loosen each string several turns with the string winder, starting with the high E and working down. After they're fairly slackened, carefully snip them with your string cutters, again working from the high E on down. With the strings removed, this is a prime time to clean that fretboard, which is described on page 13.

SEPARATION ANXIETY?

Some players prefer not to remove all six strings at a time, instead changing strings one or two at a time and thus retaining tension on the neck throughout the process. This is a subject of great debate, as many guitar techs regularly remove all six strings and receive no complaints from their employers. Other than the fact changing one or two strings at a time may take a bit longer and make cleaning a bit more tedious, there's really no difference in the process described.

The first step is to secure the string at the bridge end. This is done on most guitars by threading the string through a hole so that the ball end will catch. On Fender-type guitars, this is done through the back plate, while on Gibson-types, it's done on the back side of the bridge.

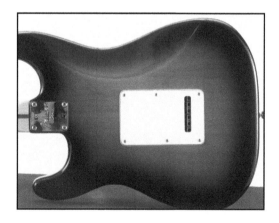

Insert string here

Now it's time to attach it to the tuning peg. There are many ways players like to do this, but here are two common methods that work well.

METHOD A (commonly used for wound strings)

1. Run the string straight through the posthole and then back out about three or four inches, so you have some slack with which to work.

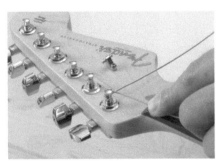

2. Wind the tuning peg with the left hand while applying tension on the string with the right hand, and on the first time around, wind on top of the string end.

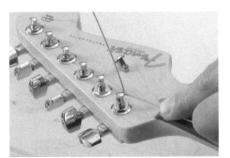

3. Next, bend then string against the post so that it's sticking up.

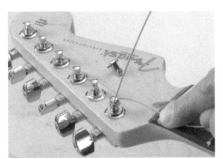

4. Continue winding the tuning peg and applying tension, but this time wind below the string end.

5. Continue winding the tuning peg while applying tension until the string is up to pitch.

METHOD B (commonly used for all strings)

1. Run the string straight through the posthole and then back out about three or four inches, so you have some slack with which to work.

2. Wind the tuning peg about ¼ turn, so that the string end is sticking out the side.

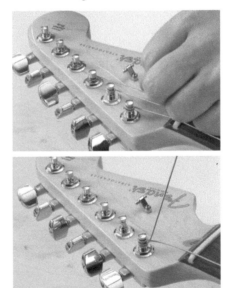

3. Next, pull the string end back *behind* the tuning post and hook it underneath the string at the post. In other words, you're taking the long way back to the string at the post. Once it's hooked underneath, give it a sharp bend upward.

4. Now wind the tuning peg with the left hand while applying tension with the right hand until the string is up to pitch. Since we're winding right against the string end, this is a great locking tie.

Method B is the one I use unless I anticipate having to remove and reinstall a set of strings repeatedly. It works great for normal stringing, but if you remove them and put them back on too many times (as is sometimes done during a setup), they tend to break.

STRETCHING IMPROVES FLEXIBILITY

Aside from applying tension while you wind your strings, stretching them out is an absolute necessity if you'd like to avoid going flat for days. Just give a good strong tug along the length of each string, and repeat the process until they hold their pitch after the stretching. If you're a player that bends strings regularly, you'll be quite happy you spent the five extra minutes on this step!

ACOUSTIC GUITARS

The method for attaching strings at the headstock is the same as with an electric, but the bridge attachment is different. Most acoustics use bridge pins for this purpose.

The bridge pin has a little cutout on one side of the tube, and it's important that you aim that cutout toward the fretboard. You want the ball end of the string to sit snugly up against the bridge plate on the underside of your guitar's top, and that cutout in the bridge pin serves as the guide.

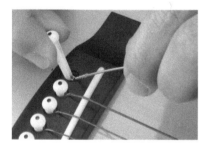

Insert the ball end of the string into the bridge hole, followed by the bridge pin with the cutout facing forward (toward the fretboard). Don't shove the string far down the hole yet.

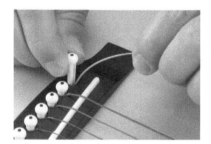

Using the bridge pin as a guide, begin pushing the ball end of the string down into the hole. Once the bridge pin is about halfway down, you should be able to pull the string back up so that it sits against the underside of the bridge.

Once you feel the string seated against the underside, finish inserting the bridge pin so that it's flush with the bridge top.

If you make a habit of installing strings this way, your guitar will likely hold its tuning better, and your bridge will last a long time.

CLEANING & POLISHING

It doesn't take too much effort to keep your guitars looking sharp for years and years. Before we talk about any cleaning products or techniques however, let's start simple. Rule #1: Always wash your hands before you play! Not only will your instrument feel better and therefore play better, you'll increase the life of your strings significantly. If you make it a habit of immediately picking up your guitar after fixing your car or eating some fried chicken, it will make the task of cleaning that much more difficult.

Cleaning the Body

Martin guitar
polish

Fender polish cloth

To clean the body, start with a slightly damp cloth to get all the surface dirt off. You can use a cotton or a cotton flannel T-shirt if you don't have a cotton cloth. Once you've done that, you can apply a variety of cleaning products for a more thorough cleaning, such as guitar polish, naphtha (lighter fluid), or other liquid cleaners. Work in circles all over the body, and then buff and polish with a dry rag or a polishing cloth.

Cleaning the Fretboard

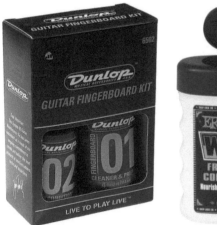

Dunlop Guitar Fingerboard Kit

Ernie Ball
Wonder Wipes

As mentioned earlier, the first step in keeping a clean fretboard is washing your hands before you play. Beyond that, you can usually get by with a cleaning routine each time you change your strings. If you gig often, you may want to clean the fretboard after every few shows. (Of course, you may end up changing strings that often anyway, depending on your preference.)

You can start with a damp cloth if you'd like, or you can begin with one of the many fretboard cleaners available. There is some debate over the use of certain products, such as lemon oil or steel wool (to clean the frets). However, there are numerous products by reputable companies that will do the job just fine. If you make a habit of cleaning regularly, you'll never need more than a rag, a cleaner, and a bit of elbow grease to do the job.

Kyser
Dr. Stringfellow

Fingerease

There are also plenty of string-cleaning products available, such as Fingerease. With consistent hand-washing, I haven't found a need for these products, but feel free to give them a try. I do know players that swear by them.

HOW OFTEN SHOULD I CLEAN?

This really depends on how often, and for how long, you're playing your guitar. If you're up there sweating out three or four sets, you'd do wonders to simply wipe off the guitar with a damp cloth after every gig, applying a more thorough cleaning when you change strings. If you only play a few times a week in the comfort of your air-conditioned bedroom, you can probably get by just cleaning the body and fretboard with each string change.

That's pretty much all there is to it. People can make quite a fuss over cleaning, but it's really not that involved. As long as you don't let your guitar go for months and months (or years!), you'll do fine with the many products readily available at any music store.

STORAGE & CARE

Humidity has a very real effect on guitars—especially new acoustic guitars. After the first four or five years, the effects become less noticeable, but you can still damage your guitar if you subject it to severe circumstances.

Hot, humid summers do affect your guitar. You may notice a bit higher action and a slight change in tone on acoustics. You can adjust your setup if this bothers you too much. However, it's the dry winters that are the real problem. When guitars dry out, the wood shrinks. This can manifest in protruding frets and, in worst-case scenarios, cracks in the finish.

The first degree of protection is to keep the guitar in its case when you're not playing it. The better solution is to maintain a good level of humidity during these months. A humidifier that's religiously filled with water will work well. There are also a number of guitar-specific humidifier products that fit inside your guitar or case. Be sure to pay close attention to the directions when using these products, as they're not fool-proof!

Planet Waves
acoustic guitar humidifier

SKB
guitar humidifier

As for the rest of the elements, such as animals, people, and the like, common sense is your best deterrent. Don't leave your guitar lying on the floor unless you'd like it stepped on, and don't lean it precariously against the wall; it's not a matter of *if* it'll fall—just when. If you're not done with your playing session, put the guitar in a stand until you're ready to play again. This simple rule will undoubtedly save your prized instrument from a needless battle scar.

CHAPTER 3: SETTING UP AN ELECTRIC GUITAR

It's quite amazing what a good setup can do. The first time you play your guitar after it's been setup well, it can feel like a different instrument. It will play more comfortably and more in tune than ever before, which is likely to inspire you to actually play better. When we setup a guitar, we're adjusting, among other things, the action (how high the strings are off the fretboard) and the intonation (how well the guitar plays in tune). Let's take a general look at what's involved in setting up an electric guitar.

BASIC ELEMENTS OF AN ELECTRIC GUITAR SETUP

Neck Adjustment: This is done by adjusting the truss rod.

String Height: This is done by adjusting the string saddles or the bridge, depending on the guitar.

Nut Adjustment: This is done by filing the nut slots (if strings are too high) or shimming/replacing the nut (if strings are too low).

Pickup Height: This adjustment makes more of a difference in tone than many players realize.

Intonation: This will help your guitar play in tune better at all places on the neck.

PRELIMINARY INSPECTION

The first thing we should do is simply inspect the guitar to make sure everything is tightened properly. On the headstock area, this includes the string trees, the nuts around each tuner on the front side, the screws securing the tuners on the back, and the screws at the end of each tuning key. You should also check the pickups, the output jack, the strap buttons, and the volume knobs to make sure they're securely fastened. If you discover anything that's not snug, you should tighten it up (acquiring a new part if necessary) before proceeding.

NECK ADJUSTMENT

The next thing is to see if the neck needs adjustment, which is done via the truss rod. The *truss rod* is a long metal rod that runs through the neck designed to counter the string tension. On most guitars, it's accessed where the headstock meets the neck. Some guitars have a truss rod plate that needs to be removed. Most truss rods are adjusted with an Allen wrench, though others require a nut driver or a flathead screwdriver.

MORE SEPARATION ANXIETY!

Other truss rods are accessed at the other end of the neck, where it meets the body. For these types of guitars, unfortunately, you need to remove the screws that hold the neck onto the body. This is a big detractor for many people, but it really needn't be. A "bolt-on" neck is just that; it's bolted (or screwed) onto the body. Removing it won't do any damage.

In order to make the proper truss rod adjustment, we need to know whether the neck is bowed too far one way or the other. If it's too far forward, the strings will be too high off the fretboard, making the guitar difficult to play and causing tuning problems. If it's too far backward, you'll get string buzz all over the place.

Here's what you can do to check. Make sure you're tuned up to pitch.

1. Place a capo on fret 1.

2. Next, press the low E string down at around fret 17 with your right hand.

3. Now take your feeler gauges and measure the distance between the bottom of the low E string and the top of fret 8. This distance should be approximately .010 inches, or .25 mm.

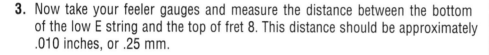

If the distance is much different than that, you'll need to adjust the truss rod. If your distance is *less* than .010 inches, you need to *loosen* the truss rod by turning counter clockwise. If the distance is *greater* than .010 inches, you need to *tighten* the truss rod by turning clockwise.

CAUTION: EASY DOES IT!

When making truss rod adjustments, take it slowly. *Always* loosen a bit first. If it happens that a truss rod is extremely tight already, it could break if you tighten it anymore. If the rod seems excessively tight, try spraying some WD-40 on it. Once you've determined that there is some play available, make your adjustments in small increments—no more than an eighth or quarter turn at once.

Remember that the truss rod shouldn't be used to set action. If the neck is bowed forward, the action will obviously be higher, but that shouldn't be your method for raising action; that's done at the bridge. The goal with the truss rod is to get the neck nearly straight (with just a *slight bit* of relief, or forward bow).

After each adjustment, retune to pitch and take your measurement again. It wouldn't hurt to wait five or ten minutes before making another adjustment if necessary. Once you get the neck adjusted properly, you can move on.

STRING HEIGHT

Ok, once you've got the neck adjusted, it's time to set the string height at the bridge. Place a capo on fret 1, and then use your 6" ruler to measure the gap at the twelfth fret between the bottom of each string and the fret.

The generally accepted norm for this measurement is 3/64th–1/16th of an inch (1.2 mm–1.6 mm). Your preference may be slightly different, but this is a good place to start. If the gap is too much or little on a particular string, you need to adjust the height of that string at the bridge.

Fender Style Guitars

On a Fender or something similar, this is done by adjusting individual string saddles with a small Allen wrench—usually a 1.5mm. There are two screws for each saddle; make sure you adjust each to the same height.

Gibson Style Guitars

On a Gibson style, we don't have individual saddles to adjust. We're only able to adjust the height of the entire bridge with two outside screws. This is done via two thumb screws or slotted screws. If we need to adjust the height of a specific string, our only real option is to file the individual string saddle.

Floating Tremolos

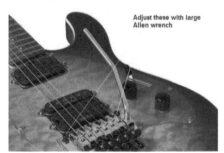

Adjust these with large Allen wrench

On a floating tremolo bridge, such as a Floyd Rose or a Kahler, we can again only adjust the overall height of the bridge. This is done with an Allen wrench.

We do have another method of adjusting the individual saddles on a floating tremolo though. You can use shims that are designed to fit underneath the saddles. If one of the saddles is measuring too low, you can place a shim beneath it to raise it to the correct height. But what if all six saddles are measuring too high? If this is the case, you probably need to lower the entire bridge. It should be basically flush with the body.

Once we've got all six strings at the correct height, it's time to move on.

NUT ADJUSTMENT

The next step is to check the string height at the nut. We'll use our feeler gauges for this as well. Some people prefer to do this by feel, but that usually requires a bit more experience. Therefore, the gauges are helpful in the beginning.

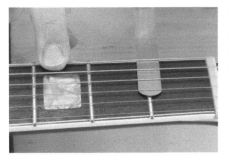

Begin with the low E string, and push down at fret 3. Now take your feeler gauges and measure the gap between the string and the *first* fret. This should be about .005 inches, or about .13 mm. Repeat this for each string, and jot down the distance for any string where the gap differs significantly from this measurement.

If the gap between the string and first fret for any string is too wide, you need to file the nut slot with a special tool called a *nut slotting file*. The files are different sizes to accommodate the different-sized slots. Nut slotting files can be a little pricey (usually between $70 and $150 for a set of six), so if you don't plan on using them often, it may not be worth it to you, considering you'll usually pay less for a setup. But they're great to have if you've got a DIY mentality and anticipate working on your guitars for years to come.

Remove the string completely, or detune it to provide plenty of slack and move if off to the side. Gently file at a slight downward angle toward the headstock. Stop and take measurements often; you can always take more off.

If the gap between the string and first fret is too narrow on any string, you're likely to get buzzing when you play notes on that string, or even the open string itself. If this bothers you, you'll probably need to shim the nut or replace it altogether. Nuts are not expensive at all, but you may want to have a qualified repairman handle the job if you don't feel comfortable.

IF YOU'RE "NUT" TOO TIMID

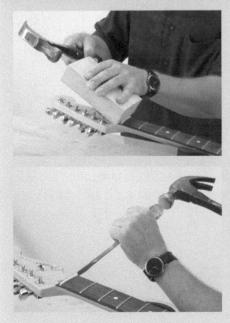

As with any repair, you need to be cautious when removing a nut, but remember that they were designed to be a replaceable part (otherwise they wouldn't be so easily removable). First, use an exacto knife to carefully score every surface where the nut touches. Then, you can use a block of wood, placed flush with the nut, and tap it lightly with a hammer. It's best to tap mostly toward the body of the guitar, as it's possible to chip off the small piece of fretboard between the nut and headstock. When tapping toward the headstock, tap very lightly.

After it's been loosened with this approach, you can usually get it out sideways by using the hammer to lightly tap a small flathead screwdriver against the nut.

If the nut will still not come out after this, it's probably been glued with a type of superglue or an epoxy that requires more force to break. You should take it to a qualified repairman in this instance, as they'll most likely have to cut through the middle of the nut and collapse it to get it out.

If you do remove the nut, you can easily make a shim out of a business card. Just glue the bottom of the nut to the card with Elmer's glue, and then trim the excess around the nut.

After it dries, you can put the nut back in place and take your measurements again. As long as you have too much gap between the string and first fret, you can glue your shimmed nut into the slot (Elmer's is fine again) and then file the nut slots if necessary.

PICKUP HEIGHT

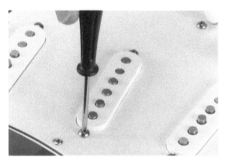

Next, we'll adjust the pickup heights. Some people have different preferences on this, but we'll use a middle-of-the-road measurement that satisfies most. Using your 6" ruler, adjust the pickup screws so that the distance from the bottom of the string to the pickup is as follows:

Single Coils	Treble Side	Bass Side
Bridge pickup	3/32"	1/8"
Middle pickup	3/32"	1/8"
Neck pickup	1/8"	5/32"
Humbuckers		
Bridge pickup	1/16"	3/32"
Neck pickup	1/16"	3/32"

"STRATITIS": NO LAUGHING MATTER!

Ok so the name sounds funny, but if you've ever experienced the phenomenon, it's *extremely* frustrating (a fine time to put that hammer to use on the wall!). The short of it is this: With some single-coil pickups, if you raise them too close to the strings on the bass side, you may experience a warbled, buzzing tone wherein the string sounds as though it's out of tune with itself. This is most noticeable when playing the low E string high up on the neck, as it's the thickest string and is closest to the pickup magnet here.

Some pickup magnets are so strong that they interfere with the string's natural vibration, causing all kinds of havoc. If you're experiencing any of these symptoms on your guitar, try lowering the bass side of the pickups to see if it goes away. If it does, you can raise them until you just start to notice the phenomenon, and then back them off a little.

INTONATION

Intonation adjustment is the last step in a guitar setup, since every other aspect (save for the pickup height) would likely alter the intonation. When we adjust the intonation, we're essentially changing the length of each string by moving the individual string saddles forward or backward. The goal is to make the harmonic at fret 12 the same exact pitch as the fretted note there. Here's how we do it. Beginning with the low E, repeat the following procedure for each string:

1. Using your tuner, tune the twelfth-fret harmonic to the note E. (A strobe tuner will give a more accurate reading, so use it if you have one. Otherwise, a standard tuner, combined with your ear, will get you pretty darn close.)

2. Now, fret that E note and check the tuning. Be sure to press straight down so you're not bending the string. If that note matched the harmonic perfectly, then that string is intonated, and you can move on to the next string.

   - If the fretted note was flat, then you need to move the string saddle forward so that it's closer to the neck.

   - If the fretted note was sharp, you need to move the string saddle back, so that it's farther from the neck. On a Fender type guitar, you do that with a Phillips screw located at the back of the bridge. On a Gibson style, you also adjust a screw on the rear of the bridge (though it's occasionally on the front). These are usually flathead screws.

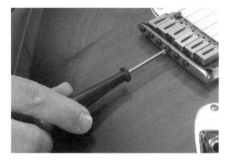 

3. Next, tune the harmonic once more (moving the saddle will throw it off) and then recheck the fretted note. Continue adjusting the saddle until the two match.

INTONATING A FLOATING TREMOLO

Adjusting the intonation on a floating tremolo, such as a Floyd Rose, is a bit more time-consuming and irritating. You must unlock the saddles before you can adjust them. The problem, and the source of frustration, is that if you do this with string tension still applied, the saddle will jut forward from the tension. Therefore, the string must be slackened before you unlock the saddle.

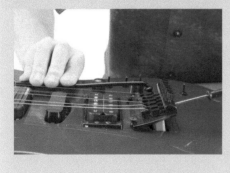

Most people do this by detuning (remember to unlock the nut!). However, another way is to press down the whammy bar (as if dive-bombing). This requires a bit of coordination, but it's quicker. Once the string is slackened, you can loosen the attachment screw and move the saddle forward or backward, retighten it, retune, and check the intonation. Most likely, you won't have gotten it right the first time, and you'll have to repeat this process many times.

In the event that you've moved the saddle as far as you can one way, and you're running into the attachment screw, you can move the attachment screw to another hole to make more room for adjustment.

Once all six strings are intonated properly, you're done. Your guitar should be singing like new or better!

CHAPTER 4: SETTING UP AN ACOUSTIC GUITAR

With an acoustic guitar, we have less control over the setup than with an electric guitar. We don't usually have moveable parts on an acoustic. (Many archtops do have adjustable bridges, but we'll be concentrating on flattops here.) A very expensive guitar is likely to be setup very well straight from the factory. (At least we'd hope so!) If you can't afford a $3,000 Gibson or Martin, however, don't fret. There are several adjustments we can make to improve the performance of many guitars. Let's take a look at the basic elements of an acoustic guitar setup.

BASIC ELEMENTS OF AN ACOUSTIC GUITAR SETUP

Neck Adjustment: This is done by adjusting the truss rod.

String Height: This is done by making adjustments to the saddle.

Nut Adjustment: This is done by filing the nut slots (if strings are too high) or shimming/replacing the nut (if strings are too low).

Intonation: Though we don't have nearly as much control as on an electric, we can make minor adjustments by shaping the saddle a bit.

PRELIMINARY INSPECTION

The first thing we should do is simply inspect the guitar to make sure everything is tightened properly. On the headstock area, this includes the nuts around each tuner on the front side, the screws securing the tuners on the back, and the screws at the end of each tuning key. You should also check the strap buttons to make sure they're securely fastened. If you discover anything that's not snug, you should tighten it up (acquiring a new part if necessary) before proceeding.

NECK ADJUSTMENT

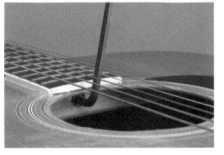

The next thing is to see if the neck needs adjustment, which is done via the truss rod. *The truss rod* is a long metal rod that runs through the neck designed to counter the string tension. On acoustic guitars, it's usually accessed where the headstock meets the neck or at the neck-body joint by reaching just inside the soundhole. Most guitars have a truss rod plate at the headstock that needs to be removed if the access is there.

Most truss rods are adjusted with an Allen wrench, while others require a special truss rod tool, which is basically a nut driver with an angled handle.

In order to make the proper truss rod adjustment, we need to know whether the neck is bowed too far one way or the other. If it's too far forward, the strings will be too high off the fretboard, making the guitar difficult to play and causing tuning problems. If it's too far backward, you'll get string buzz all over the place.

Here's what you can do to check. Make sure you're tuned up to pitch.

1. Place a capo on fret 1.

2. Next, press the low E string down at around fret 17 with your right hand.

3. Now use your feeler gauges to measure the gap between the bottom of the low E string and the top of fret 7 or 8. There should be a tiny crack of light—about .010–.012 inches.

If the distance is much different than that, you'll need to adjust the truss rod. If your distance is *less* than .010 inches, you need to *loosen* the truss rod by turning counter clockwise. If the distance is *greater* than .010 inches, you need to *tighten* the truss rod by turning clockwise.

CAUTION: EASY DOES IT!

When making truss rod adjustments, take it slowly. *Always* loosen a bit first. If it happens that a truss rod is extremely tight already, it could break if you tighten it anymore. If the rod seems excessively tight, try spraying some WD-40 on it. Once you've determined that there is some play available, make your adjustments in small increments—no more than a quarter turn at one time, but an eighth of a turn is better if you have the patience.

Remember that the truss rod shouldn't be used to set action. If the neck is bowed forward, the action will obviously be higher, but that shouldn't be your method for raising action; that's done at the bridge. The goal with the truss rod is to get the neck nearly straight (with just a *slight* bit of relief, or forward bow).

After each adjustment, retune to pitch and take your measurement again. It wouldn't hurt to wait a few minutes before making another adjustment if necessary. Once you get the neck adjusted properly, you can move on.

STRING HEIGHT

Once you've got the neck adjusted, it's time to set the string height at the bridge. Place a capo on fret 1, and then use your 6" ruler to measure the gap at the twelfth fret between the bottom of each string and the fret.

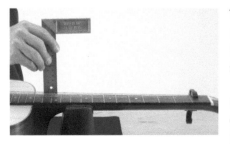

The generally accepted norm for this measurement is 3/64th–1/16th of an inch (1.2 mm–1.6 mm). Your preference may be slightly different, but this is a good place to start. If the gap is too much or little on a particular string, you need to adjust the height of that string at the bridge.

On an acoustic guitar, we don't have the flexibility we do on an electric, because we don't have individual string saddles; we only have one big string saddle. Therefore, we can only make somewhat rough adjustments. You'd be surprised how effective we can be, however.

If all six strings are measuring too much gap, *and your guitar does not have a piezo pickup*, you can simply remove the strings (and capo), remove the saddle, and sand it at the bottom to remove the height. Be sure to sand with a flat surface; that means either use a sanding block or place a piece of sandpaper on a table and sand on top of it. If you just hold a piece of sandpaper in your hand and sand freely, you most likely won't be sanding flat, even if you think you are.

You can start with a medium grade, such as 120 grit, and follow up with a finer grade. The medium grade will be responsible for removing the height, while the finer grade is used to achieve a smooth, uniform surface. Remember to only remove a little bit at a time. You can always take more off, but it you shave too much off, you'll have to get a new saddle. Shave off a little, smooth it out, reinstall the saddle, restring and capo, and take your measurements again. You may have to repeat this process ten or fifteen times.

If only a few strings are measuring too high, then you'll need to shave off the top of the saddle where those strings rest, doing the best you can. Depending on the discrepancy, and which strings are measuring high, you may be better off getting a new saddle. They're not expensive, and the radius should be pretty close, assuming you get a suitable replacement. Then you can just shave off the bottom if necessary to reach the appropriate height.

If all the strings are measuring too low, you'll either need to get a new saddle or shim the current one. It's quite easy to make a shim from a business card; the process is the same as when shimming the nut (see page 24).

WHAT ABOUT A PIEZO PICKUP?

Remember we said not to shave off the bottom of the saddle if you have a piezo pickup. There's a good reason for this. The piezo crystals are very sensitive to the saddle's vibration, and when the guitar comes from the factory, the bottom of the saddle is (assumedly) making perfect, even contact with the pickup. By sanding the bottom of the saddle, even most carefully, you will more than likely upset this delicate balance. The result will likely be an uneven string response from your pickup. Therefore, on guitars with piezo pickups, you should always make height adjustments to the saddle by sanding the top surface.

NUT ADJUSTMENT

The next step is to check the string height at the nut. We'll use our feeler gauges for this as well. Some people prefer to do this by feel, but that usually requires a bit more experience. Therefore, the gauges are helpful in the beginning.

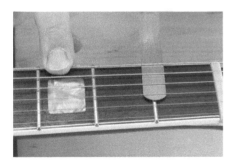

Begin with the low E string, and push down at fret 3. Now take your feeler gauges and measure the gap between the string and the first fret. This should be about .005 inches, or about .13 mm. Repeat this for each string, and jot down the distance for any string where the gap differs significantly from this measurement.

If the gap between the string and first fret for any string is too wide, you need to file the nut slot with a special tool called a *nut slotting file*. The files are different sizes to accommodate the different-sized slots. Nut slotting files can be a little pricey (usually between $70 and $150 for a set of six), so if you don't plan on using them often, it may not be worth it to you, considering you'll usually pay less for a setup. But they're great to have if you've got a DIY mentality and anticipate working on your guitars for years to come.

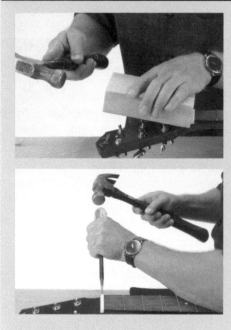

Remove the string completely, or detune it to provide plenty of slack and move if off to the side. Gently file at a slight downward angle toward the headstock. Stop and take measurements often; you can always take more off.

If the gap between the string and first fret is too narrow on any string, you're likely to get buzzing when you play notes on that string, or even the open string itself. If this bothers you, you'll probably need to shim the nut or replace it altogether. Nuts are not expensive at all, but you may want to have a qualified repairman handle the job if you don't feel comfortable.

IF YOU'RE "NUT" TOO TIMID

As with any repair, you need to be cautious when removing a nut, but remember that they were designed to be a replaceable part (otherwise they wouldn't be so easily removable). First, use an exacto knife to carefully score every surface where the nut touches. Then, you can use a block of wood, placed flush with the nut, and tap it lightly with a hammer. It's best to tap mostly toward the body of the guitar, as it's possible to chip off the small piece of fretboard between the nut and headstock. When tapping toward the headstock, tap very lightly.

After it's been loosened with this approach, you can usually get it out sideways by using the hammer to lightly tap a small flathead screwdriver against the nut.

If the nut will still not come out after this, it's probably been glued with a type of superglue or an epoxy that requires more force to break. You should take it to a qualified repairman in this instance, as they'll most likely have to cut through the middle of the nut and collapse it to get it out.

If you do remove the nut, you can easily make a shim out of a business card. Just glue the bottom of the nut to the card with Elmer's glue, and then trim the excess around the nut.

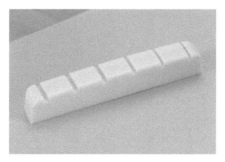

After it dries, you can put the nut back in place and take your measurements again. As long as you have too much gap between the string and first fret, you can glue your shimmed nut into the slot (Elmer's is fine again) and then file the nut slots if necessary.

INTONATION

Ideally, the intonation on an acoustic guitar should be set properly at the factory. We have even less control over intonation on an acoustic than we do over the string height. Having said this, there are still slight adjustments we can make that do make a difference.

Intonation adjustment is the last step in a guitar setup, since every other aspect would likely alter the intonation. When we adjust the intonation on an acoustic guitar, we're basically limited to changing the length of each string by slightly reshaping the saddle. The goal is to make the harmonic at fret 12 the same exact pitch as the fretted note there. Here's how we do it. Beginning with the low E, repeat the following procedure for each string:

1. Using your tuner, tune the twelfth-fret harmonic to the note E. (A strobe tuner will give a more accurate reading, so use it if you have one. Otherwise, a standard tuner, combined with your ear, will get you pretty darn close.)
2. Now, fret that E note and check the tuning. Be sure to press straight down so you're not bending the string. If that note matched the harmonic perfectly, then that string is intonated, and you can move on to the next string.
   - If the fretted note was flat, there's really not too much we can do about it. If we try to file that portion of the saddle so that the length of the string is shorter, we'll most likely be lowering the string height as well.
   - If the fretted note was sharp, we'll file that portion of the string saddle so that the string is lengthened, meaning it makes contact at the saddle farther away from the soundhole.

Take notes of which strings were sharp and by how much. This is all a matter of estimates, so you can either write notes such as "barely sharp," "very sharp," or, if you have a strobe tuner, list the amount of cents that a string is sharp. Make small pencil marks on the saddle that the surround the string that needs adjustment.

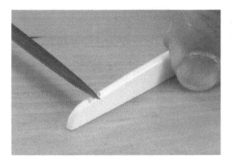

After that, remove the saddle, and, with a file lying flat, begin filing over that string section toward the back of the saddle. You should be filing from low (at the front, or neck side of the saddle) to high (at the back side of the saddle). The goal is to make the string contact the saddle farther from the neck than it did before, while affecting its height as little as possible. Again, take your time with this. Make small adjustments, then reinstall the saddle, restring, retune, and check the intonation again. Repeat the process until the harmonic and fretted note match, or until you get as close as you can.

CHAPTER 5:
BASIC ELECTRONIC REPAIRS & MODIFICATIONS

Many players are unnecessarily afraid of opening the hood and messing with the electronics inside the guitar. The truth is, there's almost no damage you can do that can't easily be undone—oftentimes you'll end up making improvements in the process. With a little common sense and a bit of studying, you can easily make repairs or modifications to your guitar's wiring that would run you hundreds at the shop. We'll look at three common problem areas in electric guitars: the output jack, the pickups, and the volume/tone pots.

TOOLS

All three of these will most likely require the use of a soldering iron, so if you don't have one, you'll need to acquire one. You can handle pretty much any job with a 25- or 30-watt model like you'll find at a hardware store or Radio Shack. You'll also need some 60/40 resin-core or rosin-core solder, which is available at the same places.

Desoldering tools are also quite handy. These are used to clean up solder blobs or remove solder in order to detach a wire. I recommend a *desoldering pump*, or a "solder sucker," which works quickly and effectively. Once the solder is molten, you cock the solder sucker, aim the opening at the solder, and then press the release button to suck up the solder. A *desoldering bulb* works similarly with a vacuum action. You squeeze the bulb, then place the tip to the excess solder and release the squeeze.

    A *desoldering braid* (or wick) is another option. Though I find them more difficult to work with, there are times when it's hard to reach the work with a solder sucker, and the braid fits the bill better. Once the solder is molten, place the end of the braid into it so that the excess solder flows onto the braid. Clip off the used portion of the braid and repeat the process if necessary.

A soldering iron stand is another nicety, as the little wire stands that often come with a soldering iron are woefully inept. These are available as basic stands and full-blown "soldering stations," which contain other goodies too.

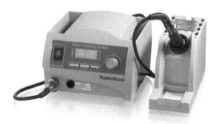

If you're the DIY type, you can make a stand for your iron with a block of wood, a coat hanger, and a weight of some sort (I used two heavy chain links). Simply drill a hole in the wood and slip a straightened-out coat hanger into it. Place a bit of Gorilla Glue at the mouth of the hole before you insert the coat hanger so that it will be held securely. After the glue dries, wind the coat hanger into a spiral with the aid of some pliers. Attach some form of weight to the front of the block of wood (you could alternatively screw it into a table for a fixed installation), and you're done!

Additionally, you should keep a damp sponge near your soldering iron stand. Commercial stands will often have a spot for these. This allows you to dab the tip and keep it clean throughout the job. A damp kitchen sponge placed into a small tray with a bit of water will work just fine.

SOLDERING AND DESOLDERING WIRES

Soldering is an easy task that can be fun as well. (At least I find it that way!) Here's a quick primer on how to solder successful connections that will last for decades.

If you're using a basic 25-watt soldering iron, it probably won't have an on/off switch. You simply plug it in, and it begins to heat up. It usually takes about four or five minutes to reach its working temperature. **Use caution; soldering irons are hot! Don't grab them by anything other than the handle, or you could suffer a nasty burn**.

Before you start working, you should "tin" the tip. "Tinning" is the process of getting a bit of solder on the tip, which allows for better heat transference. Simply uncoil a bit of solder so it sticks out several inches in a straight line and apply a bit to the tip, twisting the iron as you do so the entire tip is covered. You'll know right away if your iron is hot enough; the solder should begin to melt pretty much instantly once it touches the tip. (Not only does solder get hot very quickly; it also cools very quickly—usually in a matter of seconds.)

When soldering a wire to a terminal, there's a proven technique for getting quality results every time. First, try to get a good physical connection before even applying the solder. This means wrapping the wire around the terminal and clamping it down. Small needle-nose pliers are perfect for this work.

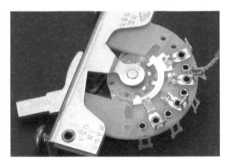

Once a good physical connection is achieved, you will then solder the connection. First, apply the soldering iron to the connection. In other words, touch the terminal just next to where the wire is wrapped. This will heat the area. Give this a few seconds (depending on the wattage of your iron), and then apply the solder to the connection—not to the iron. The solder should flow into the connection.

Once the solder begins to flow and adequately covers the area, remove the soldering iron first and then remove the solder wire. The whole process should take about five seconds or so. The solder will continue to flow for a second or so after you remove the iron, and if you don't remove the solder wire in time, it will harden with the solder and be stuck to it. If that happens, you'll need to either clip it off with wire cutters (if a little extra solder is not a big deal), or reapply the iron to liquefy the solder once more.

If the wire moves while the solder is cooling (which only takes three or four seconds), you should repeat the process until the wire remains steady. Otherwise, you risk a "cold joint"—a solder connection in which a pocket of air remains. This is not good for conductivity and often results in malfunction in the future, if not immediately.

WIRE TO WIRE

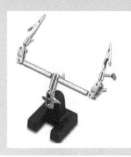

Soldering one wire to another (for instance when you need to extend the length of a wire) is a tricky proposition without the help of a device called a "third hand." If you've ever tried soldering one wire to another without one, you know what I mean. They're relatively inexpensive ($10 or $15), but they're very handy to have around.

If you end up applying too much solder, and things get out of hand, just use the solder sucker or braid to clean up the excess and start again. You don't need a lot of solder for a strong connection, but it should be solid. Once the solder has cooled (give it ten seconds just to be sure), you should be able to give a good tug·on the wire without it coming loose. It's a good idea to practice soldering on some dummy items (a jack, a 5-way switch, etc.) before tackling a real project.

OUTPUT JACK

Common problems players encounter with the output jack include scratchiness, an intermittent signal, or no signal. All of these problems are usually easy to fix, and the really good news is that, in the event that you can't fix it, it's easy and cheap to install a brand new jack.

UNDER THE HOOD: THE OUTPUT JACK

If you've never taken a peek inside, here's what a typical output jack looks like. Electronically speaking, there's no difference between an input jack and an output jack. They're just means of getting a signal to pass from the internal components of a device or instrument to a cord. Guitars use a standard quarter-inch mono jack (unless it's a stereo guitar). One of the terminals carries the hot signal, and the other is routed to ground. If just one of the wires is not making solid contact with its terminal (or it's mistakenly making contact with both terminals), the jack will not operate properly.

tip   sleeve (shield)

A standard, quarter-inch guitar cable is equipped with a TS plug, which stands for tip-sleeve (or tip-shield). The tip carries the hot signal, and the sleeve connects to ground. When the cable is inserted into the jack, the tip makes contact with the hot terminal, while the sleeve makes contact with the ground terminal.

If you're experiencing problems with the output jack, here's what to do:

Unplug the guitar and remove the screws necessary to access the output jack. (On a Strat, the output jack has its own casing on the front, whereas on a Tele or Gibson style, the jack is located on the bottom of the body.) Carefully pull out the jack wiring assembly; pull slowly so you don't disconnect anything. Inspect the two wires first to see if they're making solid contact with the terminals. If they're not, you'll need to re-solder them. (See "Soldering and Desoldering Wires," page 26.)

ground

hot

If the wires look good, try plugging in a guitar cord (make sure the other end's not plugged into anything) and check to see if the tip and sleeve are making good contact with the terminals. It could be that the jack terminals are bent out of place. If this is the case, you should be able to bend them back with a pair of pliers. If you're not able to, desolder the wires (refer to page 27) and rewire a new output jack. Assuming the wires are connected to the pots properly, you'll only need to connect the ends of the wires to the new jack. Remember to match the hot wire with the hot terminal and the ground with the ground. In most guitars, a black wire will be used for ground, whereas a white or red wire will be used for hot. However, you should double-check the wiring diagram for your guitar to be sure (see page 31). Refer to "Pickups" for more on wiring diagrams.

If both the terminal and the wires look good, the problem is most likely at the other end of the wires, or the jack could be corroded. Try spraying the jack terminals with DeOxit. If that doesn't take care of the problem, you should wire in a new jack.

PICKUPS

Changing pickups is one of the easiest modifications you can make to your guitar that can significantly alter the tone. It's a fairly easy operation that anyone with some basic soldering skills can perform. First off, remove the strings. Though it's possible to change pickups without removing the strings, it's much easier to just not have to deal with them. Once that's done, it's time to open the hood.

Strat Style

On a Strat, unscrew the pickguard and carefully lift it up. It will be connected by only a few wires running in the output jack and possibly the tremolo spring cavity, so take note of them. Turn the pickguard assembly upside down, making sure not to strain the connecting wires.

Make a note of where the pickup wires are going for the pickup you want to replace. The hot wire will be mounted to one of the terminals at the 5-way (or 3-way) switch, while the ground wire will most likely be connected to the back of a potentiometer, or pot, along with several other ground wires.

Draw a diagram of what you see, and take a picture with a digital camera if you have one. Once you're certain you know how the new pickup will replace the old one, it's time to remove the old pickup. Unscrew it, and then desolder the wires from the switch and ground connection. Be careful not to burn any surrounding wires while you're desoldering! If it will be difficult to remove the grounding wire without desoldering any other grounding wires in the process, just simply clip the old pickup's grounding wire near the grounding connection.

Screw your new pickup into place and solder the new wires. Remember, the hot wire runs to the switch; the grounding wire will likely run to the back of a pot. There should be directions with your new pickup that will indicate which wire is which.

Tele Style

A Tele is similar to a Strat, except that, instead of removing the pickguard, you need to remove the knob plate on the front to access the wiring cavity. The pickup wires reach the wiring cavity through small channels.

From there, the process is the same. Diagram what you see and photograph it, unscrew and desolder the old pickup, and wire in the new pickup.

Gibson Style

The wiring for a Gibson style guitar is accessed by removing a panel on the back. Similarly to the Tele, the pickup wires arrive to the main cavity via smaller channels.

The main difference between the Fender and Gibson design with regards to pickup wiring is that the hot wire on Gibson guitars runs to a pot instead of the switch. (The pot then runs to the switch.) The grounding wire, as with Fenders, usually runs to the back of a pot.

Other than that, the process is the same. Diagram what you see and photograph it, unscrew and desolder the old pickup, and wire in the new pickup.

SAMPLE WIRING DIAGRAMS

Provided here for reference are wiring diagrams for stock versions of a Fender Stratocaster, a Fender Telecaster, and a Gibson Les Paul.

Fender Stratocaster (three single coil pickups, 5-way switch)

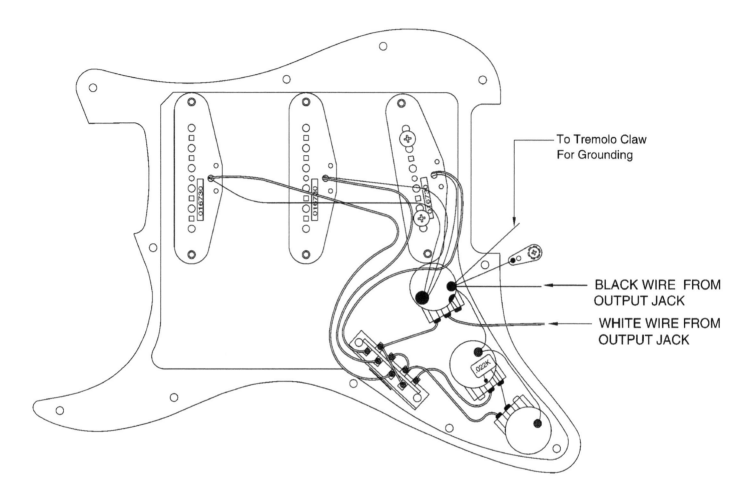

To Tremolo Claw
For Grounding

BLACK WIRE FROM
OUTPUT JACK

WHITE WIRE FROM
OUTPUT JACK

Fender Telecaster (two single coils, 3-way switch)

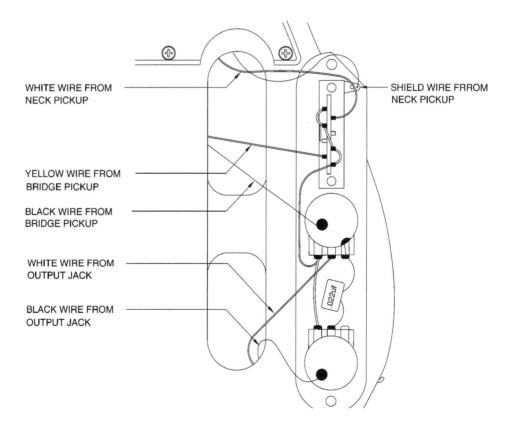

WHITE WIRE FROM
NECK PICKUP

YELLOW WIRE FROM
BRIDGE PICKUP

BLACK WIRE FROM
BRIDGE PICKUP

WHITE WIRE FROM
OUTPUT JACK

BLACK WIRE FROM
OUTPUT JACK

SHIELD WIRE FRROM
NECK PICKUP

2 Humbuckers, 2 Volumes, 2 Tones
3 Way Switch

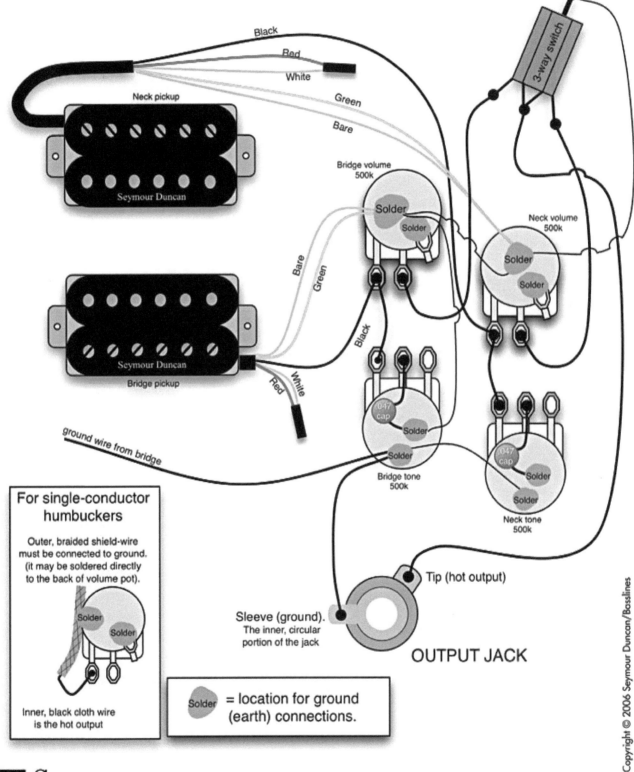

For single-conductor humbuckers

Outer, braided shield-wire must be connected to ground. (it may be soldered directly to the back of volume pot).

Inner, black cloth wire is the hot output

Solder = location for ground (earth) connections.

 **Seymour Duncan**®
5427 Hollister Ave. • Santa Barbara, CA. 93111
Phone: 805.964.9610 • Fax: 805.964.9749 • Email: wiring@seymourduncan.com

AFTERWORD

Well, there you have it. By now, you should be armed with the knowledge and tools to turn that clunker into a real hot rod. I hope you've enjoyed this journey into the inner workings of the guitar; I certainly enjoyed being your guide. And though we only scratched the surface of the electronic side of things, I hope the veil has been sufficiently lifted so that you're able to glimpse a clearer picture of what's going on in there. The potential for modifications is vast to say the least, and with a little knowledge and perseverance, you'll be able to turn your instrument into the one you've always wanted.

I wish you the best of luck in your future tweaking and tinkering. Feel free to drop me a line at chadjohnsonguitar@hotmail.com.